COOKING
★ WITH ★
GAS

★ JEAN NEL ★

RWF

CONTENTS

Best-selling author of *Braai the Beloved Country*, Jean Nel is back with his considered and expansive book on getting the best out of your gas braai. Originally trained in the hotel trade, Jean quit that branch of the hospitality industry to pursue a career in catering.

It wasn't long before this Karoo farmer's kid started driving his catering business in the direction of outdoor cooking with fire. He has been cooking in the open, on wood- or gas-fuelled fires for as long as he can remember. Whether it's a Weber kettle, some bricks and a grid, or one of those newfangled gas contraptions you see all over these days, as long as it has a flame, Jean will cook you something delicious on it.

To this day, whether he's teaching or catering for large corporate launches on some mountain-top or in the desert with his beloved Webers, Jean never fails to turn up for his regular slot at the Stellenbosch Slow Market. His renowned 'Flamed' stall has been feeding the Saturday crowd straight from the grill for almost a decade, and he's a much-loved, flamboyant fixture among seasoned traders and new visitors alike. If you pop by and order a braaied breakfast in a bun, you may even talk him into signing one of his books.

– Russel Wasserfall

I've been cooking on open fires for a long time. A very long time. I admit I was a bit of a purist, insisting on making a fire a certain way every time, but when I moved from cooking socially to catering and using a braai as a work tool, I moved to what many in the Braai World would consider sacrilege – gas!

Why, you may ask? The answer for me is very simple – convenience. Gas braais are far more convenient to operate than wood or charcoal braais. That's why a leading brand of braai units – or barbecues – saw a 40 per cent rise in gas braai sales in 2013 alone. Gas braais are simple and convenient to use, and they are much cleaner to operate.

For me the deciding factor was the fact that you just switch the thing on, set the heat and it will stay there for hours. If the flame dies, it's because you've run out of gas. Just swap the cylinder and carry on working. When you're cooking for hundreds at a market or function, you can't be running back and forth with firewood and live coals. Gas is the answer.

Of course there's an argument that rages in certain circles about whether coals or a gas flame is the better heat source. The most important point that I think emerges from the debate is that a gas flame cannot achieve the heat you can get out of wood or charcoal fires. It's true. Coals provide greater heat, which is what you want for that perfect steak or chop that's rare in the middle and crispy-charred on the outside. However, there are ways to achieve that with gas and if you look at the long list of other advantages gas offers, that one point holds very little water.

What we use to run our gas braais is known to the initiated as LPG. I've heard some pretty interesting guesses at what that stands for, but basically it is liquid petroleum gas. Elsewhere it is called propane or butane and it is essentially a mixture of flammable hydrocarbon gases.

One of the moans I hear often from the "Woodies" is that gas imparts an unpleasant flavour to whatever you cook with it. Nonsense. I've spent an entire career cooking on both and I'm prepared to stand up and be counted on that one. You are more likely to get flavour-taint on food from excessive use of firelighters. Gas braais as well as wood every time.

Essentially, a gas braai is a stove. You get to use it outdoors though, which is my favourite place to cook. With that go-anywhere, can-do versatility comes a lot of advantages for the outdoor cook. It heats up quickly, so you can start cooking in 10 minutes, and you can control the temperature with a dial. That's it in a nutshell – cooking with gas offers convenience and control.

Not only are you able to set a very specific temperature on a gas braai, you can maintain a desired temperature until the gas runs out. I've got a 9 kg bottle on my gas braai, and it can last me up to 6 months of cooking three or four days a week. Wood and charcoal fires, on the other hand, have a very limited lifespan. You can burn more on the side and keep feeding your coal-bed, but that's a lot of work when the alternative is simply cooking with gas. All you need to do is go out to the braai and push the button. Click-click! One spark and you're cooking with gas. The real allure of this is that you can cook on a gas braai every day. The unit you invest in will become an extension of the kitchen to be used all week long. It won't be something you haul out of the garage once a week or once a month. No more dirty hands and disposing of ash.

In this book, I set out to guide the novice through the various skills and tricks you need to learn to cook a perfect braai using a gas unit. Starting with some pretty obvious stuff, the recipes take you from searing a lamb *tjop* right through direct and indirect cooking to all the trendy new braai stuff like salt-block cooking and planking. Basically I'm setting out to give you the one must-have recipe book that you must buy with your shiny new gas braai.

Practice – The first rule about cooking with gas is that you have to practise. Cooking is a skill that you need to work on a little bit. Using a gas braai takes a lot of the mess and fuss out of the process, but cooking the perfect roast or steak doesn't come naturally. You can cook on one a couple of times a week and, with this book as a guide, you'll be an expert in no time.

Temperatures – With practice you will get to know your gas braai. Considering the range of models available, I can't tell you: "Set it on #1 for fish and #3 for steak." You need to work that out for yourself by trial and error. In the recipes I indicate low, medium, medium-high or high for the temperatures settings. Fiddle a bit with the dials – usually they go from 1 to 5 or there's some sort of scale.

Weather – Heat can vary with the weather. A hot setting might burn food on a sunny day, but gently singe it if it's windy outside. The more you practice the better you'll get to know your braai, and how it performs in different conditions.

Thermometers – That thermometer on the hood can be important, especially for indirect cooking. They are not precise, as lids seldom seal tightly, but they serve as a guide. If you tend to roast at between 180°C and 200°C in your domestic oven, something around that temperature is what you want for the gas braai. Again, trial and error is the answer. To be precise, you could use a good digital oven thermometer, but I've never needed one.

Preheat – Cooking with gas does require just a little patience. As convenient as it is, you can't just push the clicker and slap a steak on the grill. It needs a little time to heat up. You wouldn't heat an oven for baking or roasting with the door wide open. So shut the lid to raise and maintain the heat.

Zones – If your gas braai has two or more burners it is easy to have two heat zones. You want somewhere to cook, and somewhere to move food to when it's done, or getting too scorched.

Oil – When you are placing anything, particularly meat, on the grill, you need to oil it first. This is to stop stuff sticking like boerewors to a braai-grid. I place a little vegetable oil in a ramekin and paint the oil on with a basting brush. Go easy, you don't want big flare-ups. Do this a few minutes before cooking.

Season – Whenever I say salt and pepper in a recipe, I am referring to flaked salt and freshly ground pepper unless otherwise specified. (There are one or two instances where good old white pepper is the only thing that will do the trick.)

Unclog – Apart from the obvious absence of cinders and ash, cleaning a gas braai is a doddle because drips usually vaporise. They do get carbon and grease build-ups that need to be scraped or washed away every once in a while though. Gas jets can also clog up. Use a toothpick to make sure all burner holes are clear of debris. Clogged burners result in a low flame and heat levels will drop dramatically. A healthy braai will last a long time – so keep it clean.

Meat – Get to know your butcher. He will guide and help you select your produce for the braai. Chatting with him regularly will guide you to better, interesting cuts and even give you great cooking tips.

Heat – One of the common complaints about gas braais is that they don't get as hot as coals. I like a steak crunchy on the outside and pink in the middle. You need to work a little to get this right, but the first rule is: Keep the lid closed! Critics will moan that this steams the meat, but I invite them to try one of my steaks. A closed lid keeps things hot and the heat works its magic.

Some fancy gas braais have 'infrared' burners where a gas flame superheats a ceramic or metal plate that radiates much more heat than standard burners. It achieves the kind of temperatures that steakhouses cook at. Great if you can afford it, but trust me, we've got it covered.

Done – Lastly, I refuse to cook meat to well-done stage. I think it ruins the experience, and it's disrespectful to good ingredients. The recipes all have times or methods for medium-rare. If you want to burn it – go for it.

Serves – The recipes in this book are designed to serve 4 to 6 people. In a few instances, like with planked salmon, the portion guide is how many people you think you can feed with the piece of meat indicated. If there are more of you, pop another piece on the barbie.

CLICK-CLICK

This is the start-up section. It's the chapter where you unwrap your shiny new gas braai and cook your first chop on it. If you want to avoid actually being a chop, read the instructions that come with your braai. There are usually some basic assembly instructions included, and you need to connect your new baby to a gas bottle. There are reasons manufacturers or retailers recommend certain gas bottles of a certain size or capacity. It's best to go along with those, especially if this is your first gas braai.

In the following pages we will look at the basic use of your braai, looking to season it and build up your confidence making recipes that require the direct cooking method. There's no hidden meaning here, it's where you put something on a braai grid and it gets cooked by direct heat from the plates, grids or lava rocks which are in turn heated directly by the gas flame.

We start with some basic recipes before moving on to the indirect cooking method for slightly more involved dishes, and then we look at the latest trends in braai technique.

First though, we need to season the braai – run it in if you like – by cooking a few simple things on it. The idea is that you want to be able to use the gas braai as much as possible. I have friends who cook on theirs every night. They make their sides and veggies, get everything ready and then pop out to the braai and cook a lovely piece of chicken or a steak. Practice is the key to cooking with gas, so the more you use your braai, the better cook you will be. The convenience of hitting the button, hearing the click-click and cooking something for dinner means that you are not limited to using it on social occasions. Dinner for two is just as easy as cooking on a kitchen stove, and it just tastes better.

★ GREEK ★ LAMB CHOPS

INGREDIENTS

8 large lamb chops,
trimmed of excess fat

salt and pepper

30 ml dried oregano

15 ml dried mint

4 gloves garlic, crushed

zest and juice of 2 lemons

Perfectly braaied lamb chops are a showstopper. You want a contrast between a juicy pink centre and a nice char on the outside. You need heat to get a crispy crust, so get the braai to medium/high heat. Work your tongs, turning it when it is seared. Make sure the lamb chops are around the same weight/size so they cook at the same rate. Weight is one guide here, but so is size and thickness.

Place the lamb chops in a shallow dish and season with salt and pepper. Crush the dried oregano, mint and garlic cloves in a mortar and pestle, and pound to a rough paste, or whizz them in a food processor. Stir in the zest, lemon juice and olive oil. Pour over the lamb chops and turn to coat. Cover with some plastic wrap and marinate for 3 hours. Remove from the refrigerator an hour before cooking.

Braai the lamb chops on a medium to high heat for 5–6 minutes, turning once.

★ LAMB ★ SOSATIES

INGREDIENTS

1 kg deboned leg of lamb
1 small garlic clove, crushed
4 bay leaves
15 ml ground ginger
8 ml ground coriander
60 ml milk
15 ml salt
15 ml pepper
1 onion
250 ml dried apricots
5 ml cornflour
6 metal skewers

Trim the excess fat and skin off the lamb. Cut into 4 cm cubes. Place the lamb pieces in a bowl with the garlic, bay leaves, ginger, coriander, milk and seasoning. Mix well. Cover and refrigerate overnight.

Peel the onion and cut it into wedges. Thread the cubed lamb, dried apricots and onions onto the skewers. Pour the leftover marinade into a pan, bring it to the boil and leave to simmer for 2–3 minutes. Mix the cornflour with 15 ml cold water, stir it into the sauce and simmer gently for a few more minutes. Keep sauce warm.

Bring your braai to a medium to high heat, oil the grid and start cooking your lamb sosaties, turning twice. The lamb sosaties should be nicely browned, but still pink in the centre. Serve with the thickened marinade as a sauce.

★ TANDOORI ★ CHICKEN THIGHS

INGREDIENTS

500 ml double cream yoghurt

30 ml fresh lemon juice

30 ml fresh ginger

60 ml minced garlic

15 ml ground coriander

15 ml turmeric powder

15 ml salt

8 ml cayenne pepper

8 ml freshly ground black pepper

8 ml ground cumin

8 bone-in chicken thigh pieces

oil for brushing

60 ml butter, melted

chopped coriander leaves

1 red onion, thinly sliced

Puree 250 ml yoghurt, lemon juice, ginger, garlic, coriander, turmeric, salt, cayenne pepper, black pepper and cumin in a food processor until smooth. Transfer to a bowl and stir in the remaining yoghurt. Add the chicken pieces and turn to coat. Cover and refrigerate overnight.

Remove chicken from fridge 30 minutes before the braai. Set your braai on medium. Brush the grid with oil. Remove the chicken pieces from marinade. Braai for about 12 minutes per side, turning once. Baste chicken with the leftover marinade and melted butter during the last 4 minutes of cooking.

Remove chicken from the braai and garnish with chopped coriander leaves and sliced red onion.

OLIVE OIL AND LEMON ★ CHICKEN ★

INGREDIENTS

4 chicken breast fillets

60 ml olive oil

60 ml fresh lemon juice

salt and pepper

When choosing your chicken pieces, try to make sure they are of roughly even size. Just as with steak or anything else you cook, if they are of uniform thickness and weight, they will cook at the same rate.

Place the chicken in a shallow bowl. Pour the olive oil, lemon juice and seasoning over it and leave it, covered, for 30 minutes. There's no need for any overnight marinating – the point about this recipe is that it's quick and easy. Half an hour after you get home from the shops, you can be cooking.

Remove the chicken from the marinade. Heat your gas braai to a medium heat. Braai the chicken breast fillets for 8–12 minutes turning once. Serve sliced with a fresh, crisp salad.

CAESAR ON THE BRAAI

INGREDIENTS

4 skinless chicken breast
fillets, trimmed

sea salt and pepper

60 ml olive oil

6 bacon rashers

½ loaf ciabatta, sliced

cos lettuce, separated and
washed

anchovy fillets, to serve

shaved Parmesan, to serve

DRESSING

1 garlic clove

4 anchovy fillets

8 ml sea salt flakes

60 ml finely grated Parmesan

1 egg yolk

30 ml white wine vinegar

15 ml Dijon mustard

125 ml olive oil

A Caesar salad made on the braai is a beautiful thing. It's sophisticated and pretty, but it also has that lovely scorch from the grid.

To make the dressing, pound the garlic, anchovy and sea salt in a mortar and pestle to a paste. Add the grated Parmesan, then whisk in the egg yolk, vinegar and mustard. Gradually whisk in the oil until incorporated.

Preheat gas braai to medium. Brush the chicken with oil, and season with salt and pepper. Braai for 5 minutes on each side, until just cooked through. Set aside to rest for 5 minutes. Braai the bacon rashers until cooked to your satisfaction. Place the sliced ciabatta on the braai grid, and toast both sides lightly. Slice into cubes or tear into bite-size pieces.

Put the lettuce leaves in a large bowl. Drizzle with the dressing, season with salt and pepper and toss well. Slice the chicken breasts (across the grain), add to the bowl with the ciabatta croutons and crispy bacon and toss gently. Serve the salad topped with anchovy fillets and shaved Parmesan.

INGREDIENTS

6 x 400 g T-bone steaks
vegetable oil for brushing
salt and pepper
200 g salted butter
4 cloves garlic, finely chopped
handful of flat-leaf parsley,
chopped

The T-bone steak is king of the steaks and marvelously easy to braai. It incorporates a piece of sirloin, full of flavour, and a bit of fillet, nice and tender. Season it well ahead by brushing it lightly with vegetable oil and seasoning both sides with salt and pepper.

While the braai is heating, place the butter, garlic and parsley in a heavy-bottomed pan to one side of the braai. Putting cold butter on cooked steaks is a no-no. Rather let it heat gently on the side of the grill so the flavours can infuse.

When the braai is as hot as you can get it, sear the steaks on both sides. Now braai for 2–3 minutes on each side until medium-rare. Do not move the steaks, but close the lid between turning them. Transfer the steaks to a plate and let them rest for 5 minutes. Spoon the warmed garlic butter over the T-bones.

You can vary the butter flavours with different herbs. Mashed anchovy fillets with butter is my favourite.

★ SIRLOIN ★
WITH A CHIMICHURRI SAUCE

INGREDIENTS

4 x 250 g sirloin steaks

salt and pepper

olive oil for brushing

CHIMICHURRI SAUCE

(Makes about 500 ml)

125 ml red wine vinegar

5 ml salt

3 garlic cloves, minced

45 ml finely chopped white onion

1 red chilli, finely chopped

500 ml chopped coriander

250 ml chopped flat-leaf parsley

80 ml chopped fresh oregano

200 ml olive oil

Cooking a steak without the bone is easier, as you don't have to watch for very rare spots close to the bone. It's also easier to eat in a polite fashion with a knife and fork.

Chimichurri is a bright green sauce that is a staple condiment in Argentina. It's a blend of olive oil, fresh herbs, garlic, chilli and red wine vinegar that pairs very well with beef. It is awesome on chicken, hard cheese and loads of other stuff too. To make it, combine vinegar, salt, garlic, onion and chilli in a bowl and let it stand for 10 minutes. Stir in the coriander, parsley and oregano. Whisk in the oil then pour about half the sauce over the steaks as a marinade. Cover and chill for 3 hours.

Remove the meat from the refrigerator an hour before cooking. Pour off the marinade and pat the meat dry with some kitchen paper, then season. Get the gas braai as hot as possible, oil the grid, then sear the steaks on one side before turning and cooking for 2 minutes. Turn again and cook for another 2–3 minutes for medium-rare. Serve with the remaining chimichurri.

INGREDIENTS

600 g minced beef

½ red onion, finely chopped

15 ml HP sauce

30 ml Dijon mustard

45 g fresh breadcrumbs

2 eggs

salt and pepper

4 slices mozzarella cheese

pickled cucumbers, thinly sliced

lettuce leaves

4 bread rolls, sliced in half

Making your own patties gives you control over what goes into your burger. It all starts with the meat which should be a ratio of 80 per cent meat to 20 per cent fat. Why fat? Because fat equals flavour. As I said in the introduction, you want to get to know a good butcher and he can guide you with selection.

Place the beef mince, onion, HP sauce, mustard, breadcrumbs and eggs in a large bowl and season with salt and pepper. Mix until well combined, then divide into four equal portions. Gently shape into four patties, making a small indentation with your thumb in the centre of each. This prevents it from forming a bulge once you put it on the grid. Place on a baking tray, cover with plastic wrap and refrigerate for 20 minutes.

Preheat your gas braai to a medium-high heat, and braai for 4–5 minutes each side. Do not press it down with a spatula, you will dry it out. Rest the patties for a couple of minutes before assembling the burger of your dreams with cheese, pickles, sauces and a soft bun.

BOEREWORS ★ BAGUETTE ★ WITH ONION RELISH

INGREDIENTS

45 ml unsalted butter
2 red onions, thinly sliced
15 ml brown sugar
30 ml balsamic vinegar
4 x 100 g piece boerewors
oil for brushing
1 long baguette
45 ml butter
rocket leaves
15 ml olive oil
15 ml balsamic vinegar

Melt the 45 ml butter in a saucepan over low heat. Add the onion and cook, stirring for about 10 minutes. Add the brown sugar and vinegar, and continue to cook over low heat for 10 minutes. Take it off the heat. Cool down.

Preheat your gas braai to medium-high heat. Brush the grid with oil. Braai the boerewors pieces for 7–8 minutes, or until they are cooked through.

Slice the baguette down the middle, and spread with butter. Toss the rocket leaves with balsamic and olive oil, and place on the baguette. Top with the boerewors and onion relish.

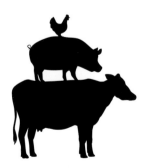

★ CHILLI SALT ★
KUDU LOIN

INGREDIENTS

2 x 200 g piece kudu loin
butter for brushing

CHILLI SALT

90 ml salt
30 ml black peppercorns
15 ml chilli flakes
15 ml fresh rosemary, chopped
olive oil
1 lemon, halved

Pound the salt, black peppercorns, chilli flakes and rosemary in a mortar and pestle. Rub the meat with some olive oil and coat it with the spice mix.

Preheat your gas braai to high. Braai the kudu for 6 minutes per side or to your liking. Brush with melted butter when you take it off the braai and squeeze half a lemon over the meat. Let it rest for 5 minutes before you slice it. Serve with the other lemon half for seasoning.

PORK CHOP
★ WITH MRS BALL'S ★ CHUTNEY MARINADE

INGREDIENTS

4 pork chops, 2 cm thick

salt and pepper

oil

MRS BALL'S CHUTNEY MARINADE

120 ml olive oil

250 ml Mrs Balls Chutney

60 ml lemon juice

60 ml orange juice

60 ml Worcestershire sauce

30 ml wholegrain mustard

15 ml sweet chilli sauce

1 clove garlic, crushed

salt and white pepper

Mix the ingredients for the marinade together in a bowl and pour over the pork chops in a non-metallic bowl. Leave for one hour.

Preheat your gas braai to high. Brush the grid with oil. Take the pork chops out of the marinade and season with salt and pepper. Braai for 6–8 minutes, turning once. Baste with the leftover marinade while it cooks.

INGREDIENTS

800 g pork fillet, cut into 2 cm cubes

30 ml smoked paprika

3 garlic cloves, finely chopped

125 ml sherry

30 ml olive oil

15 ml sage, chopped

salt and pepper

metal skewers or wooden skewers soaked in water

Put the pork cubes in a non-metallic bowl. Combine the smoked paprika, garlic, sherry, olive oil, sage and seasoning in a small bowl. Make sure the smoked paprika dissolves, and pour over the pork to coat well. Cover and refrigerate for up to 6 hours. Remove the pork 30 minutes before you braai.

Thread cubed pork onto the soaked wooden skewers or metal skewers. Preheat the gas braai to medium. Braai pork kebabs for 8 to 10 minutes, turning every 2 minutes. Pork kebabs should have a golden colour. Remove from the heat and rest for 5 minutes.

Serve with buttery rolls.

PORK SAUSAGE
★ WITH ORANGE BASTING ★

INGREDIENTS

45 ml orange marmalade
30 ml orange juice
15 ml balsamic vinegar
4 x 100 g pork sausages

Place the marmalade, orange juice and balsamic vinegar in a pan, heat up and stir until it is runny. Let it cool down. Put the room temperature sausages in the pan with the basting sauce and leave them for 20 minutes. When I cook this, I actually start heating the sausages in the pan on the braai grid. They are very delicate and tend to burst their skins if you apply heat too quickly. Once they start to colour, I transfer them straight to the grid on a medium heat. Braai them for 6–8 minutes, turning often for even colour, until cooked through. Spoon the leftover marmalade, basting over the sausages before serving.

BRAAIED FISH AND CHIPS

INGREDIENTS

4 red-skinned sweet potatoes, cut into wedges

30 ml olive oil

salt and pepper

15 ml chilli paste

200 ml mayonnaise

30 ml fresh lemon juice

30 ml coriander leaves, chopped

4 x 175 g tuna or yellowtail

Drop the sweet potato wedges into a pot with lightly salted water. Bring to a boil and simmer for 8–10 minutes. Drain the sweet potatoes and toss them in olive oil. Season with salt and pepper. Braai them on a medium to high heat until crispy and golden.

Mix the chilli paste with the mayonnaise, lemon juice and chopped coriander and set aside.

Crush the peppercorns in a mortar and pestle, rub it into the tuna steaks. Place the tuna steaks onto the oiled grid and braai for just under 2 minutes per side (depending on thickness of steaks). Season with salt.

Pile the chips onto a platter then place tuna stakes on top. Serve it with the mayonnaise.

★ MOROCCAN SPICED ★ SWORDFISH

INGREDIENTS

2 x 200 g swordfish steaks

oil for brushing

MOROCCAN SPICE MARINADE

250 ml chopped coriander leaves

2 cloves garlic, crushed

15 ml ground cumin

15 ml paprika

15 ml ground coriander

15 ml lemon zest

30 ml fresh lemon juice

45 ml olive oil

Blend all marinade ingredients in a food processor. Brush the swordfish steaks on both sides with some marinade, place in a non-metallic dish, cover and refrigerate for 30 minutes. Heat your braai to a medium-high heat. Braai the fish for 10–12 minutes, turning once until cooked through. Brush the fish with marinade about half way through cooking each side.

MEDITERRANEAN VEG PLATTER

INGREDIENTS

1 red pepper, sliced in quarters

1 yellow pepper, sliced in quarters

1 large aubergine, cut into thick slices, then in half again

2 large baby marrow, cut diagonally

4 baby fennel bulbs, cut into 6 cm slices

1 red onion, cut into wedges

HERB, LEMON AND GARLIC MARINADE

2 sprigs of rosemary

2 sprigs of marjoram

2 sprigs of thyme

2 garlic cloves, coarsely chopped

zest of 1 lemon

freshly ground black pepper

pinch of salt

250 ml olive oil

Strip the rosemary, marjoram and thyme leaves from the stalks and put in a mortar and pestle. Add the garlic and lemon zest and pound to release the aromas. Put the mixture in a bowl with the freshly ground black pepper, salt and olive oil. Set aside.

Put all the vegetables in a large bowl, add the marinade and toss gently until evenly coated. Marinate for 30–45 minutes.

Preheat the gas braai to medium–high heat. Braai the vegetables directly on the grid until they are all tender and lightly charred. Cool, then peel the peppers.

Arrange vegetables on a large platter. Garnish with any leftover fennel fronds. Drizzle with more olive oil and season vegetables again. Serve at room temperature.

BRAAIED HALOUMI
★ WITH PEPPERS AND CHORIZO ★

INGREDIENTS

2 red peppers

2 chorizo sausages, cut into 5 mm slices

pinch of smoked paprika

60 ml olive oil

15 ml red wine vinegar

250 ml chopped coriander, flat-leaf parsley and mint leaves

400 g tinned chickpeas, rinsed and drained

250 g haloumi cheese, cut into 1 cm pieces

olive oil

pinch of chilli flakes

juice of 1 lemon

Preheat your gas braai to high. Braai the red peppers, turning occasionally, for 15–20 minutes, until the skin turns black. Remove from the braai, set aside to cool. Peel, deseed, discard the skins and cut it into strips.

Cook the chorizo until blackened on each side. Add the chorizo to a bowl with the smoked paprika, olive oil, vinegar, fresh herbs, red peppers and chickpeas.

Lightly coat the haloumi with oil and braai for 1–2 minutes until golden on each side. Season with salt, chilli flakes and lemon juice. Assemble the salad with the haloumi on top and serve.

BRAAIED AVOCADO ★ AND CHILLIES ★

INGREDIENTS

90 ml olive oil

2 large red chillies, quartered and deseeded

1 red pepper, quartered and deseeded

1 yellow pepper, quartered and deseeded

2 red onions, sliced in thick slices

3 avocados, halved and pitted

salt and pepper

90 ml red wine vinegar

45 ml basil pesto

Heat your gas braai to medium. Brush braai grate with some oil. Season the chillies, red and yellow peppers and red onion with salt and pepper. Braai, turning occasionally, until softened, about 10–12 minutes. The peppers will take a little longer, up to 20 minutes, so start them first and add the rest of the vegetables after 5 minutes so they all finish at the same time. Transfer to a bowl.

Mix the red wine vinegar with the basil pesto. Drizzle over the braaied chillies, peppers and red onion.

Rub the cut side of avocadoes with 15 ml of olive oil. Season with salt and pepper. Braai, skin side down until avocado is golden brown, about 3 minutes. Arrange everything in a serving bowl or on a board and serve with a green salad as a main course, or as a side with the meat you are serving.

HEATING UP

Now that the start-up section is done, you want to move on to some of the stuff that really sets a gas braai apart from a live coal one. The shiny new gas braai should have a little mileage on it, so you are past the simple act of sticking a slab of meat on it and watching it turn into something delicious. Here's the next step.

The huge advantage of cooking with gas is temperature control. As long as your gas bottle is charged, you can set the temperature on your unit with a dial, and cook all night at the same temperature. Some of the recipes in this chapter put that statement to the test. When you come to something like the Pulled Beef with Passata, you will set the temperature very low and leave the beef to cook for 3 hours or more.

So a gas braai is like an outdoor oven, as well as providing you with a live fire at the touch of a clicker. To get the best out of it, we've mixed some slow-cooked recipes, some indirect cooking method ideas and a few direct ones that benefit from closing the lid.

The indirect method is basically what people do when they use a live coal Weber, or kettle braai, and make fire on two sides of the braai and cook something in the centre, where it is not directly over flame or heat. The same goes for indirect cooking on a gas unit. Most give you the ability to light only one of two, or three, or even four burners. The idea is that your meat or dish, sits on the grid with no fire below it, and the unit turns into an oven heated by convection from the live burner.

This is the bit that sorts the grown-ups from the kids. It's where your outdoor cooking matures into the ability to wow family and friends with the amazing stuff you can feed them even though you are cooking outside. My market and catering work is often a source of wonder for people who aren't used to the sort of things you can do when you're cooking with gas. In this chapter, you should warm to the idea.

★ SPICY ★
LEG OF LAMB

INGREDIENTS

1.7 kg butterflied leg of lamb, trimmed of excess fat and at room temperature

3 garlic cloves, thinly sliced

90 ml olive oil

salt and pepper

30 ml red wine vinegar

30 ml coriander leaves, chopped

15 ml mint leaves, chopped

30 ml ground cumin

45 ml lemon zest, grated

juice of 1 lemon

There's a wonderful twist to this marinade, as it's applied to the leg of lamb only after it's braaied. This helps the meat to absorb the flavours as it rests and to make it exceptionally tasty and tender. Butterflied leg of lamb is without a doubt one of the best cuts to braai. The meat is full of flavour with a good fat content to keep it moist. An average leg of lamb weighs 2.3 kg and butterflied 1.7 kg. You can easily feed 8 people with this quantity of meat.

Remove the lamb from the fridge half an hour before you braai it. Use a chef's knife to cut 15 small slits into the surface of the lamb and place a slice of garlic in each slit. Drizzle with a little extra olive oil. Season well with salt and pepper.

Place the remaining ingredients into a jug. Whisk and set aside.

Preheat the gas braai to high. Reduce the heat to medium and place the leg of lamb skin side down on the braai. Braai with the hood closed for 12–15 minutes, then turn the meat over and braai for a further 15–20 minutes with the hood closed. This should give you a medium-rare leg of lamb. Transfer to a large, shallow dish, pour over the spicy marinade mixture, cover loosely with foil and set aside to rest for 10 minutes.

★ TZATZIKI ★
LAMB SHOULDER

INGREDIENTS

1.2 kg lamb shoulder,
butterflied

60 ml olive oil

60 ml red wine vinegar

15 ml dried marjoram

3 cloves garlic, crushed

salt and pepper

TZATZIKI

½ a cucumber, peeled and
sliced into ribbons (with a
vegetable peeler)

250 ml plain yoghurt

45 ml fresh lemon juice

1 garlic clove, crushed

Mix the plain yoghurt, lemon juice and crushed garlic. Pour onto the cucumber ribbons.

Place the olive oil, vinegar, marjoram, crushed garlic and salt and pepper in a large bowl and mix to combine. Add the lamb and toss to coat.

Preheat your braai to very hot. Place lamb on an oiled grid and turn the heat down to medium. Close the lid. Braai the lamb for 8–10 minutes, turn it around and braai 6–8 minutes.

Remove the lamb from the braai and place onto a chopping board to rest. Slice and serve with a fresh tomato salad and the tzatziki.

CHILLI-CORIANDER
★ CHICKEN ★

INGREDIENTS

4 chicken breasts, skin on, bone in

30 ml red chilli, chopped

2 garlic cloves

250 ml coriander leaves

125 ml unsalted butter, softened

salt and pepper

lemon halves to serve

fresh coriander leaves to serve

Remove the chicken from the fridge and pat the skin dry with some kitchen paper.

Place the chilli, garlic, coriander and butter in a food processor and whiz to make a paste. Carefully loosen the skin from one side of each breast to form a pocket and rub some of the chilli and coriander paste on the flesh underneath. Be careful not to break the skin.

Place the chicken pieces in a foil container. Rub any remaining flavoured butter over the skin and season with salt and pepper. Cook on a medium heat with the lid closed for 35–40 minutes. Remove from the braai and let it rest for 5–10 minutes before serving.

Serve with lemons halves and fresh coriander leaves.

★ CHICKEN ★ INVOLTINO

INGREDIENTS

4 large skinless chicken breast fillets

125 ml Danish feta, crumbled

15 ml fresh rosemary

salt and pepper

30 ml olive oil

30 ml lemon rind

15 ml lemon juice

30 ml basil pesto

soaked kitchen string

Put a chicken breast between two layers of plastic wrap and pound it into an even thickness, about 5 mm. Repeat with the remaining chicken breasts. Spread crumbled Danish feta over each flattened chicken breast, followed by some rosemary sprigs or sage leaves. Season with salt and pepper. (Season lightly with salt as the Danish feta is salty.)

Gently roll up the chicken breasts, from one short end to the next, enclosing the feta and rosemary. Tie the involtino with kitchen string and put into a non-metallic dish. Repeat to make four involtinos. Combine the olive oil, lemon rind, lemon juice and basil pesto in a bowl and pour over the chicken. Cover and refrigerate for at least 2 hours.

Remove the involtinos from the fridge 20 minutes before cooking.

Preheat your gas braai to low. Place the involtinos on the grid and close the lid. Braai for 15–18 minutes, turning twice, or until golden brown. Remove from the braai, cover with some foil and let it rest for 10 minutes.

INGREDIENTS

1 whole chicken

1 375 ml can of beer

THE ULTIMATE DRY RUB

(Makes about 125 ml)

30 ml black peppercorns

30 ml yellow mustard seeds

5 ml cumin seeds

45 ml paprika

15 ml brown sugar

30 ml sea salt

15 ml garlic powder

Stir peppercorns, mustard seeds and cumin seeds over a low heat in a pan for 2 minutes. Cool down. Put into a mortar and pestle, and grind to a consistency of sea sand. Add rest of the dry rub ingredients and mix well. This dry rub will store well for up to 3 months.

Heat your gas braai to medium heat. Remember to put a drip tray directly underneath the chicken. Fill drip tray with 1 cm of water.

Rub the chicken with the rub. Remember to rub the insides of the chicken as well. Now open the beer and drink about a third of its contents. Lower the chicken onto the open beer can. As the chicken cooks, the beer will steam and create flavour and moisture. The result should be a crisp chicken on the outside and succulent on the inside.

Braai, covered, for 45–50 minutes. Remove from the braai and let it rest for 5–10 minutes.

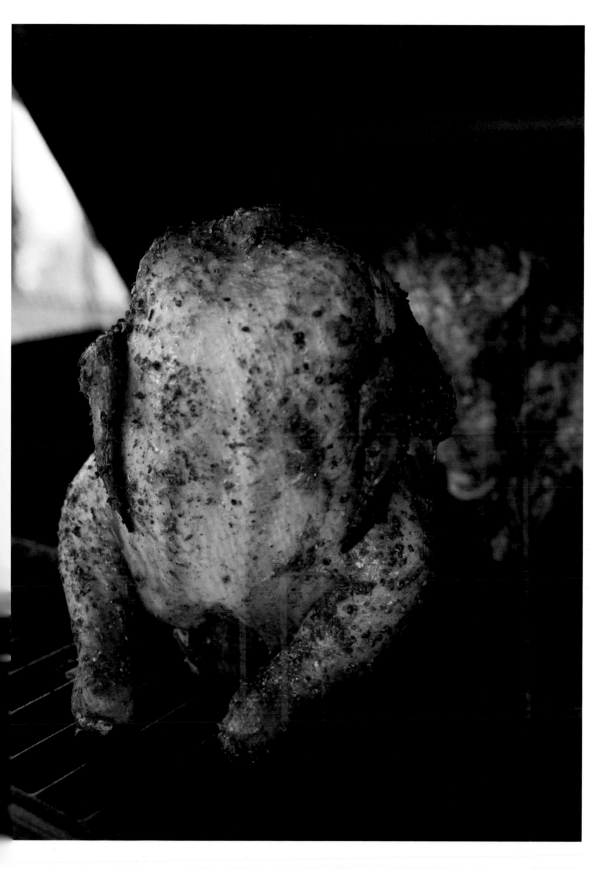

★ BRINED ★
CHICKEN

INGREDIENTS

500 ml cooking salt

250 ml white wine vinegar

15 ml fennel seeds

2 bay leaves

2 small chickens, weighing
about 1.2 kg each

Put the salt, vinegar, fennel seeds and bay leaves in a large saucepan with 10–12 litres of cold water. Bring to the boil, then reduce the heat and simmer for 25–30 minutes. Remove from the heat and allow to cool to room temperature.

Cut the chickens in half lengthways between the breasts. Immerse them in the brining solution and refrigerate for 5–6 hours or overnight. Remove the chicken, and discard the brining solution. Place the chicken skin side up on a baking tray. Refrigerate for 4–6 hours. Remove the chicken from the fridge half an hour before braaiing.

Preheat your gas braai to high and close the lid. Put the chicken skin side up over a drip tray half-filled with water. Close the lid and braai for 40–45 minutes. The skin should be golden. Remove from the gas braai and allow to rest for 10–15 minutes before serving.

WHISKEY MUSHROOM ★ RIB-EYE ★

INGREDIENTS

2 rib-eye steaks on the bone,
weighing 250g to 300g each

salt and pepper

120 ml olive oil

herb brush with sage, rosemary
and thyme

1 lemon, halved

WHISKEY MUSHROOM SAUCE

60 ml butter

1 small onion, thinly sliced

125 ml white button
mushrooms, sliced

250 ml beef stock

60 ml whiskey

60 ml pouring cream

30 ml lemon juice

15 ml finely chopped thyme

salt and pepper

Place a pan on the grid over a high heat and melt the butter. Add the onions and sauté for 2–3 minutes. Add the mushrooms and cook for 3 minutes. Add the beef stock and whiskey. Cook for 2–3 minutes. Stir through the cream, lemon juice and thyme. Bring to the boil and cook for 2–3 minutes or until thickened. Season to taste and set aside.

Season the steak with salt and pepper at least 5 minutes before you cook it. Braai for 5 minutes per side for medium-rare, brushing on a little olive with a herb brush as you go. Cover with the lid if you like a more medium to well-done steak. Remove the steak and let it rest for 5 minutes before serving with the reheated sauce poured over it.

★ HERB RUB ★ FILLET

INGREDIENTS

1 whole beef fillet, 2.5–3 kg

olive oil

8 slices white bread

Whisky Mushroom Sauce
(see page 58)

HERB RUB

30 ml fresh rosemary, chopped

45 ml salt

15 ml white pepper

30 ml fresh thyme, chopped

15 ml fresh sage, chopped

15 ml cayenne pepper

soaked kitchen string

Mix the rub ingredients in a small bowl. You can use dried herbs if you want, it actually makes the rub easier to work with, but I just prefer fresh herbs.

Trim the beef fillet of excess fat and silver skin. Place it flat on a chopping board with the smoothest side up. Neatly fold the tail of the fillet to form an even thickness. Tie the fillet together with soaked kitchen string at 4 cm intervals. Season it all over with the rub.

Heat your braai to medium to high heat. Sear the beef fillet on direct medium heat for 12 minutes, turning every 3 minutes. Now close the lid and braai indirect for 15–20 minutes for medium rare. Keep the lid closed as much as possible during this indirect cooking time. Remove from the braai, cover with foil and let it rest for 10 minutes.

While it is resting, cut out rounds from each slice of bread. Toast over medium heat on both sides.

Cut kitchen string off the fillet and carve into slices. Serve on toast rounds with the whisky mushroom sauce (page 58), or you can use your favourite pepper sauce.

★ SAUCY ★
BRISKET

INGREDIENTS

2 kg beef brisket, with a thin
layer of fat on

30 ml salt

30 ml freshly ground black
pepper

15 ml dried chilli flakes

The brisket can be seasoned with salt and pepper only;
the dried chilli flakes is optional. For this recipe, you
must braai the meat straight from the fridge – the reason
for that is the meat will absorb more smokiness – at a
low temperature between 120°C–130°C. We want an
outdoor oven so keep the lid closed. This is one of those
recipes that you start early in the morning, so it is ready
by the afternoon. It needs to cook low and slow for 4–5
hours. Leave it alone for the first 3 hours at least. If you
prod it too early, it will be hard as a rock. The process
of cooking meat like this sees it go through a miraculous
change, as it hardens first and then the tissue breaks
down so it softens totally again.

Mix the salt, pepper and chilli flakes (if using) then rub
all over the brisket. Paint the grids with a little oil. Place
it fat side down on the braai. Close the lid. Braai for
4–5 hours or until a dark crust forms around the meat.
Remove the brisket from the braai. Wrap in a double
layer of foil and braai for another hour. Remove from
braai. Let the brisket rest in the foil for another half hour.

Carve against the grain in thin slices. Serve with some
crusty bread and your favourite pickles.

PULLED BEEF
★ WITH PASSATA ★

INGREDIENTS

2.5–3kg piece of beef chuck

500 ml beef stock

2 cloves garlic, crushed

RUB

30 ml brown sugar

15 ml salt

15 ml freshly ground black pepper

15 ml ground cumin

15 ml ground coriander

5 ml mustard powder

PASSATA SAUCE

1 onion, peeled, finely chopped

olive oil

1 clove of garlic, peeled and crushed

500 ml passata

30 ml Worcestershire sauce

30 ml white wine vinegar

60 ml brown sugar

salt and pepper

1 foil tray

Remove the beef from the fridge to bring it to room temperature. Set up your gas braai at a low heat – you're looking for about 110°C. Close the lid.

Mix all the rub ingredients thoroughly in a bowl and massage the beef all over with the rub. Place the beef on an oiled braai grid on indirect heat. Close lid and braai for 3 hours. Transfer the beef to the foil tray, pour the stock around and add the crushed garlic. Cover tightly with some foil and return to the braai for another 2 hours or until the meat pulls apart easily.

For the passata, fry the onions in the oil in a large pan over medium heat. Add the garlic and fry for another minute. Reduce the heat to low. Add the rest of the ingredients. Bring to the boil, then simmer for 30 minutes or until thickened and reduced.

Serve on a platter with the passata sauce and a crusty loaf of bread. Just put it on the table, your guests will attack it.

BRAAIED PORK
★ FILLETS ★
WITH PLUM PICKLE

INGREDIENTS

2 x 400 g pork fillets, trimmed
of any excess fat

oil for brushing

250 g Chinese egg noodles

30 ml chilli-flavoured olive oil

salt and pepper

2 spring onions, sliced

chopped coriander

PLUM PICKLE

500 g plums, stoned and
coarsely chopped

1 cinnamon stick

1 red chilli, deseeded and
chopped

150 ml brown sugar

125 ml red wine vinegar

Cook the plums in a large saucepan with the cinnamon, chilli and sugar over a low heat until the sugar has dissolved. Add the vinegar, stir well and simmer for 20 minutes or until the plums are tender and the liquid has reduced. Remove the cinnamon stick. Transfer three quarters of the pickled plums to a serving dish, cover and set aside.

The pork fillets need to be cooked with both the direct and indirect method. Heat your gas braai to a high heat. Brush the pork fillets with oil and sear over direct heat for 10 minutes, turning 3 times.

Reduce your gas braai to medium heat. Baste the pork fillets with the reserved plum pickle and close the lid. Braai for a further 20–25 minutes over indirect medium heat. Baste the pork fillets throughout the remaining braai period. Remove from the braai, cover with some foil and let it rest for 5–10 minutes.

While pork fillets are resting, cook the Chinese noodles according to the packet instructions. Drain and toss in the chilli-flavoured olive oil. Season to taste. Slice the pork and put on top of the noodles, followed by the reserved pickled plums. Garnish with the spring onions and chopped coriander.

★ CARAMELISED ★ PORK NECK

INGREDIENTS

1.5 kg pork neck
1 clove garlic, sliced thinly
5 cm piece fresh ginger, sliced thinly
2 star anise, quartered
30 ml sea salt

HOT AND SWEET GLAZE

250 ml water
250 g brown sugar
4 red chillies, sliced thinly
1 star anise
90 ml soy sauce
125 ml lemon juice

Make the hot and sweet glaze by combining the water and sugar in a medium saucepan. Bring to the boil. Reduce the heat and simmer, uncovered for 10 minutes. Remove from the heat and stir in the rest of the ingredients.

Make 8–10 small cuts in the pork neck. Press garlic, ginger and star anise into cuts, rub pork with salt. Brush 125 ml of sweet glaze over pork neck.

Pre-heat your braai to medium heat. Braai pork, covered for 20 minutes. Turn pork around and braai for a further 30 minutes. Now open the lid and braai pork for a further 10 minutes. Increase heat to high and brush pork with the rest of the sweet glaze. Turn pork once the last 5 minutes. Cover pork and let it rest for 10 minutes before slicing.

INGREDIENTS

4 x 300 g lean pork chops

125 ml fresh bread crumbs

1 handful sage leaves, chopped

45 ml grated Parmesan

all purpose flour, for dusting

salt and pepper

2 eggs, whisked

vegetable oil for cooking

Trim the chops of as much fat as possible. Mix the breadcrumbs with the sage and Parmesan. Season the flour with salt and pepper. Lightly dust the pork in the seasoned flour. Shake off any excess flour. Dip pork chops into beaten egg and drain off any excess. Place pork chops into the breadcrumb mix and press down to coat evenly.

Preheat your gas braai to low. Oil the grid and braai the pork for 5–6 minutes with the lid closed, then turn over. Braai for another 5–6 minutes. Pork chops should be golden brown. You may need to pop the pork chops onto the warming rack and closed for a few more minutes.

Serve this with a green salad and braai-grilled lemons.

★ CRAZY RIBS ★

INGREDIENTS

1.2 kg pork ribs

BRAAI SAUCE

30 ml vegetable oil

2 medium-sized onions, chopped

2 garlic cloves, crushed

15 ml chilli paste

400 g tinned chopped tomatoes

90 ml brown sugar

120 ml tomato sauce

15 ml red wine vinegar

salt and pepper

Put the oil and onions in a small saucepan over low heat and cook, stirring often for 10 minutes. Add the garlic and chilli and cook, stirring, for a minute. Add the tomatoes and increase heat to high. Bring mixture to the boil. Reduce the heat and simmer for 5 minutes. Set aside to cool. Add the remaining ingredients and blend until smooth. Cool to room temperature.

Cut the ribs in half and place in a glass bowl. Pour one third of the braai sauce over the ribs and turn to coat. Cover with plastic wrap and refrigerate for 4 hours or overnight. You can also use a large re-sealable freezer bag to marinate the ribs in.

Bring the marinated pork ribs to room temperature before cooking. Preheat your braai to medium-high heat. Transfer the ribs to a foil baking tray, meaty side up. Place the tray on the flat plate, and close the lid. Braai for 45–50 minutes. Baste the ribs with the remaining sauce every 15 minutes. Finish them by turning the gas up to high, and browning the ribs directly over the fire. Heat the remaining sauce and serve with the ribs.

VEAL CUTLETS
WITH LEMON AND THYME SALT

INGREDIENTS

4 x 250 g veal cutlets (on the
bone) trimmed

sea salt

90 ml olive oil

125 ml thyme leaves

lemon wedges to serve

LEMON SALT

15 ml sea salt

zest of 1 lemon, finely grated

Pound the sea salt and lemon zest in a mortar and pestle until well combined. Transfer to a small baking tray and leave in a warm place overnight for the mixture to dry out, removing any clumps that form with your fingers.

Heat your gas braai to high. Season the cutlets with sea salt and drizzle with half the olive oil. Braai for 2–3 minutes each side, then turn them around, close the lid and braai for further 2 minutes. Use your tongs to hold the cutlets with their fatty edge on the grid for a minute to finish.

Chop the thyme finely on a chopping board, and add to the freshly ground black pepper, lemon salt and drizzle with olive oil. Place the cutlets on top of this mixture. Rest for 5 minutes.

Carve each cutlet into 4 to 5 slices and serve on the board. Drizzle with any remaining olive oil, thyme leaves and lemon salt. Serve with lemon wedges.

★ KUDU ★
CHOCOLATE-CHILLI SAUCE

INGREDIENTS

1 kg kudu loin
salt and pepper
olive oil

CHOCOLATE-CHILLI SAUCE
1 bottle of red wine (cabernet)
500 ml beef stock
30 ml brown sugar
1 red chilli, sliced
cream
100 g dark chocolate (70%)
salt and pepper

Place the wine, beef stock and sugar in a small pot on a medium-high heat. Let it simmer until it reduces in half. Add the sliced chilli and cream and simmer for 5 minutes. Take pot off the heat, and break the chocolate into the sauce. Season with salt and pepper.

Preheat your gas braai to medium-high heat. Braai the seasoned kudu loin 3 minutes on each side. Close the lid and braai for a further 5 minutes.

Let the meat rest for 5–10 minutes before you slice it. Serve on a platter with the chocolate-chilli sauce on the side or simply pour it over the kudu loin.

INGREDIENTS

1 whole fish, clean and gutted,
about 2 kg

lemon wedges to serve

THAI AROMATIC PASTE

2 garlic cloves, chopped

1 large piece of ginger,
chopped

125 ml spring onion, chopped

2 red chillies, deseeded and
chopped

1 small bunch of coriander
leaves, chopped

15 ml brown sugar

salt and pepper

15 ml tamarind paste

440 ml tinned coconut cream

Make the paste by using a mortar and pestle or a food processor. Pound the garlic, ginger, spring onion, chillies and coriander to a smooth paste. Put the paste in a bowl and add the brown sugar, seasoning, tamarind paste and coconut cream and mix to combine.

Heat your gas braai to medium. Place the fish on a piece of foil. Rub the aromatic paste over the fish, turn fish over and repeat. Wrap the fish loosely in the foil, and braai it with the lid on for 15 minutes, turning over after 7 minutes. Serve with lemon wedges.

INGREDIENTS

2 x 500g trout, cleaned and gutted

2 lemons, finely sliced

1 red onion, finely sliced

mixed fresh herbs such as dill or fennel and flat-leaf parsley

salt and pepper

Lay the trout on a clean working surface. Stuff the cavity of each trout with a few slices of lemon, red onion, sprigs of dill or fennel and flat-leaf parsley. Season the outside of the trout with salt and pepper.

Preheat your gas braai to high. Cover the grid with a sheet or two of baking paper, brush very lightly with olive oil and place the fish on this to cook. The paper conducts all the heat and you'll end up with no sticky bits or torn fish. It will colour as the fish cooks, but if the paper catches fire, your braai is too hot.

Braai for 6–8 minutes, turn the fish over and braai for another 5 minutes. The fish should be cooked to a golden colour and the skin crispy.

★ FISH ★ SANDWICH

INGREDIENTS

4 x 150 g yellowtail fillet pieces
salt and pepper
1 lemon, thinly sliced
60 ml olive oil
soaked kitchen string

DILL PESTO

375 ml fresh dill
125 ml flat-leaf parsley
60 ml pine nuts
30 ml garlic, chopped
60 ml olive oil
45 ml freshly grated Parmesan

Blend the dill, parsley, nuts and garlic in a food processor. Add the olive oil and Parmesan, and blend. Transfer to a small bowl and cover.

On a wooden board, season the yellowtail with salt and pepper. Spread the dill pesto onto 2 of the yellowtail fillets, and top with the other 2 fillets. Place slices of lemon on top and tie gently with the soaked kitchen string.

Heat your gas braai to medium heat. Oil the grid. Braai the fish fillet skin side down for 2 minutes. Turn and braai the lemon side for 3–5 minutes. Remove from braai.

★ STUFFED ★ PEPPERS

INGREDIENTS

200 g couscous

350 ml boiling vegetable stock

90 ml garlic-infused olive oil

60 ml coriander leaves, chopped

30 ml mint leaves, torn

10 baby tomatoes, halved

90 ml lemon rind, grated

250 ml feta cheese, crumbled

salt and pepper

4 red peppers

Put the couscous in a bowl and pour over the hot vegetable stock. Cover with clingfilm and leave to stand for 5 minutes, or until the stock is absorbed. Add half of the garlic-infused olive oil, herbs, tomatoes, lemon rind and feta cheese.

Cut the peppers in half, remove and discard the seeds and membranes. Brush the outside of the peppers with the remaining olive oil.

Preheat your gas braai to medium heat. Braai the peppers cut side down for 4–5 minutes. Do not turn the peppers. Remove from the braai and fill them with the couscous mixture, then return to the braai cut side up for a further 8–10 minutes.

★ AUBERGINE ★ PEPPER STACK

INGREDIENTS

2 small red peppers

60 ml olive oil

1 clove garlic, crushed

30 ml lemon juice

1 large aubergine

125 ml drained sun dried tomatoes in oil, chopped

60 g pitted black olives, chopped

125 ml fresh basil leaves, torn

200 g mozzarella cheese, sliced

60 ml basil pesto

15 ml balsamic vinegar

Halve the peppers, and discard seeds and membranes. Preheat your braai to medium. Braai the peppers skin side down until blistered and blackened. Place them in a bowl and cover with some clingfilm for 5 minutes, then peel away the skin.

Slice the aubergine lengthways into 8 slices. Discard the end pieces. Mix the olive oil with the garlic and lemon juice and brush this on the slices. Braai until you get good grid marks on each side and the flesh is just tender.

Combine tomato, olives and torn basil in a small bowl.

Place a slice of the eggplant on a serving plate, top with the mozzarella cheese, pieces of braaied red pepper and the remaining eggplant. Top with the tomato mixture. Spoon the basil pesto on each tower and drizzle with some balsamic vinegar.

★ SPINACH BLUE CHEESE ★
MUSHROOMS

INGREDIENTS

450 g spinach

15 ml olive oil

1 clove garlic, crushed

15 ml lemon juice

salt and pepper

8 evenly sized, large brown mushrooms, wiped

2 tomatoes, thinly sliced (may use baby tomatoes or just leave out)

125 g blue cheese, crumbled

Remove the large stalks from the spinach and wash well in cold water. Shake off the excess water from the spinach and chop it.

Heat half the olive oil, add the garlic and fry for a few seconds. Remember not to brown the garlic. Add the spinach and stir fry over a high heat until it wilts to the bottom of the pan. Add the lemon juice, season and mix well. Tip the spinach mixture into a colander or sieve and squeeze out the excess moisture. Transfer to a chopping board and chop finely.

Remove the stalks from the brown mushrooms, brush both sides with oil, season with salt and pepper.

Braai the mushrooms face down for about 3–4 minutes. Flip them over and quickly top with the spinach, sliced tomatoes and blue cheese. Close the hood and braai the mushrooms for a further 1–2 minutes.

COOKING
★ WITH ★
GAS

S o now you know the basics of cooking with both the direct and indirect methods on a gas braai, it's time to explore new territory. The growth of this branch of outdoor cooking has thrown up a whole lot of new techniques to play with.

Who knew Americans cooked outdoors? With fire? And they're not the only ones. Along with the growing range of gas braais, new tricks and techniques are finding their way to our braai grids. Even though only a South African can braai properly, other cultures are able to cook on fire and are teaching us a few tricks for cooking with gas.

We've got urban braai warriors smoking salmon on their braais now, or cooking on cedar planks to infuse food with a different wood flavour. Some of the stuff is pretty old stuff, like rotisserie cooking, which is just a fancy term for spit-roasting. However, there's a really cool new trend called Salt-Block Cooking and we threw in a couple of tips for that.

ROTISSERIE

The first rule about rotisserie is to forget the fancy name. It's a spit-braai, plain and simple. The scale is different, depending on the size of your cooker, but the principle is identical. Meat secured to or spiked on a spit is turned gradually over a constant heat source as it cooks.

Some gas braais come with a motorised rotisserie unit, or they're available as optional extras. Certain braai-equipment companies even manufacture stand-alone ones which may fit your gas unit. Most mid- to large-size braais have notches or openings which allow for some sort of rotisserie to operate under the hood. I tend to find the motors finicky or irritating, and there's nothing wrong with turning the spit every little while by hand.

The key to successful rotisserie cooking is moisture and flavour. The slow pace of this style of cooking allows lots of basting, which is always a good idea. Another is to make sure there is a pan of water beneath the meat so that humidity under the hood can help keep it moist.

SALT BLOCK

Salt-block cooking is the latest craze to hit the outdoor cooking scene. They are particularly useful for cooking steak on a gas braai because they absorb and radiate heat brilliantly. You get a wonderful crust on a steak from a salt block.

Salt slightly dehydrates the surface of the meat, imparting some saltiness while the temperature gets the sizzle on. You need to be watchful though, leave meat on there too long, at too low a temperature, and you will dry that puppy up like biltong. This is not a good method for anyone who likes their steak well done.

There are couple of factors to consider before using a salt block on your braai:

- Salt blocks crack if you just whack them on a high flame. Heat them slowly, by degrees, as per the supplier's instructions.
- They get incredibly hot, especially on the bottom. Use oven gloves to handle.
- Kill the flame and cool it on the braai before you move it.
- Do not place a heated salt block on your dining-room table.
- Cool salt block completely before you clean it with a sponge.

Because it absorbs fat and moisture from anything cooked on it, the block goes brown with time. It's fine though, I call that seasoning.

PLANK

Apart from its virtues in cooking and the incredible flavour it renders, planking adds beautiful colour to the crust of the food that you cook on it. Different woods impart different flavours. Planks are widely available nowadays in supermarkets, and the instructions for use are quite clear.

You're sort of smoking the food by letting the wood flavour infuse the meat. However, you don't want the plank to actually smoke by putting it over a live flame. Use the indirect method and let it warm gently and give off its seasoning as you cook your meat.

Please take into consideration that the sort of planks that can be cooked on are untreated, so don't just use any plank you find lying around at home. Soak all planks in cold water for an hour before cooking. Clean them with warm soapy water, dry and lightly oil before storing.

SMOKE

Mastering the technique of smoking salmon, chicken breasts or meats on a gas braai is easy. You will have much more success with white meats like chicken, and fish is always a winner when you smoke it. Beef is possible, but you need to use cuts that are not too thick or dense, so the smoke can infuse them.

You want to put your smoke box with the wood chips over the flame to get them smoking. Whatever you are smoking goes under the hood on the grid away from the live flame. This method is known as hot-smoking, as the smoke is warm, and the environment under that lid is hot, so the food is cooking slowly as it takes the smoke. Cold-smoking involves leading smoke from a fire into a separate chamber where the food is not exposed to heat at all.

You can buy fancy smoke boxes, but I tend to soak the wood chips in water to slow down ignition, and then put them in a little foil container. The recipes here for duck, chicken and salmon are my favourite smoked goodies.

BRICK

This is a really crazy technique and I actually laughed when someone first mentioned it to me on a course I was giving. The idea of putting a brick on top of food while you are cooking it just seemed weird. If you think about it though – and I did – it's kind of like that thing your dad used to do to get things crispy quicker.

If you press down on a burger patty or a piece of meat with a spatula, it appears to cook quicker and get a crunchier crust. I don't like it, because you are basically pressing moisture out of the meat and drying it out. In these civilised times when we like our meat a little rarer and certainly easier to chew, that's a no-no. Except that in certain instances it can work quite well.

With chicken, you get that sort of 'flattie' texture, and a crispy skin quickly. I love the method for calamari, as the tubes get a great crust and the quicker moisture loss intensifies the flavour of the dressing in the meat.

POTJIE

Ok, so it would have been remiss of me to not add a potjie recipe or two to a book on cooking with a gas braai. Honestly, the potjie story is a whole new book, as the recipes and techniques are endless. I've just put a quick teaser in here.

Essentially, as you might have learned by now, a gas braai is a big outdoor stove and oven combined. As such, cooking potjie on it is a doddle. There's no messing about with coals added one at a time, and trying to keep things constant as you cook. When you're cooking with gas, you set the temperature, pop your favourite, flat-bottomed cast iron pot on the grid, and away you go. It's still a sociable outdoor activity, but it's just so much easier. I can't think when last I cooked a potjie on live coals.

★ ROTISSERIE ★ MINT LAMB

INGREDIENTS

1 deboned leg of lamb, about
1.2 kg

salt and pepper

MARINADE

juice and zest of half a lemon

2 cloves garlic, chopped

1 spring onion, finely chopped

60 ml fresh mint, chopped

30 ml olive oil

Mix all the ingredients for the marinade in a bowl. Place the lamb in a bowl, then pour over marinade ingredients. Leave in the fridge overnight.

Bring the leg of lamb to room temperature the next day. Remove from the marinade.

Prepare your gas braai for indirect cooking.

Slide the spit gently though the leg of lamb and secure the rotisserie. Place a foil container half-filled with water directly under the leg of lamb. Turn on the motor to start the rotisserie. Cook the leg of lamb for 60–75 minutes with the lid closed. Baste the leg of lamb after every half hour. Wearing gloves, loosen the fork and slide the leg of lamb off the spit. Transfer the leg of lamb to a chopping board and allow to rest for 20 minutes before serving with sides and salad or with pita and fillings.

ROTISSERIE ★ CHICKEN ★ WITH HERB STUFFING

INGREDIENTS

1.5 kg chicken
15 ml melted butter
salt and pepper
olive oil for brushing
soaked kitchen string
1 foil container filled with water

HERB STUFFING

375 ml stale breadcrumbs
1 celery stalk, trimmed and chopped fine
1 small onion, chopped fine
15 ml rosemary, chopped
15 ml thyme, chopped
125 ml flat-leaf parsley, chopped
45 ml lemon rind, grated

Mix all the herb stuffing ingredients in a bowl. Set aside.

Remove and discard any fat from the cavity of the chicken. Fill the chicken with seasoning, followed by the herb stuffing. Do not pack herb stuffing too tightly as bread expands during cooking.

Place chicken on a wooden board, breast side up. Secure chicken with the soaked string by looping the string around the tail end, then bringing it around each end of the drumsticks. Following the creases between drumstick and body, take the string towards the wing end of chicken. Turn the chicken breast side down and secure string around wings.

Now take out the rotisserie fork. Make sure that the screws that tighten the fork are at the bottom of the spit. Spear the fork into the flesh and secure. The chickens should face the same direction if you do more than one. Place the foil container filled with water directly underneath the chicken, and braai for 60–75 minutes with the lid closed. Brush chicken with olive oil for the last 30 minutes of cooking.

Turn off the rotisserie motor, if you are not turning it by hand. Carefully remove the spit from the braai, wearing gloves. Tilt the chicken upright over the foil tray so that any liquid from body cavity can pour into the foil container. Slide the chicken from the spit onto a chopping board and allow it to rest for 10 minutes before serving.

★ ROTISSERIE ★ RUMP STEAK

INGREDIENTS

4 x 250 g rump steaks,
trimmed of fat and sinew

90 ml olive oil

30 ml dried oregano leaves

30 ml thyme leaves

15 ml rosemary leaves

salt and pepper

juice of 4 lemons

30 ml olive oil

1 foil tray

Marinate the rump steaks in the 90 ml olive oil, herbs, salt and pepper overnight in the fridge. Remove from the fridge an hour before cooking and cut into 5 cm squares.

Following the manufacturer's instructions, thread and secure the steak onto the centre of the rotisserie spit, put the spit in place and turn on the motor if you have one. Fill a foil tray with some water and place under the steak for any drippings. Close the lid. Braai the steak for 12–15 minutes. Mix the leftover olive oil with the lemon juice and baste the rump steaks every 5 minutes while cooking.

When the rump is cooked to your liking, turn off the rotisserie. Wearing gloves, carefully remove the spit from the braai. Slide the steak from the spit onto a chopping board. Allow to rest for 10 minutes before carving it.

SALT BLOCK STEAK

INGREDIENTS

4 x 200 g porterhouse steaks

RUB
60 ml salt
60 ml freshly ground black pepper
30 ml garlic salt
15 ml cayenne pepper.

Combine all the ingredients for the rub in a small bowl. Season the steaks well on both sides with this rub. Wrap the steaks individually in clingfilm and pop in the freezer for 15–20 minutes before cooking.

Heat your salt block gradually on the braai, following the instructions. You want it sizzling hot when the ice-cold steaks hit it. The idea is that you will get a good char on the outside but still have a very rare centre. Cook for about 3 minutes on each side, or to your own liking.

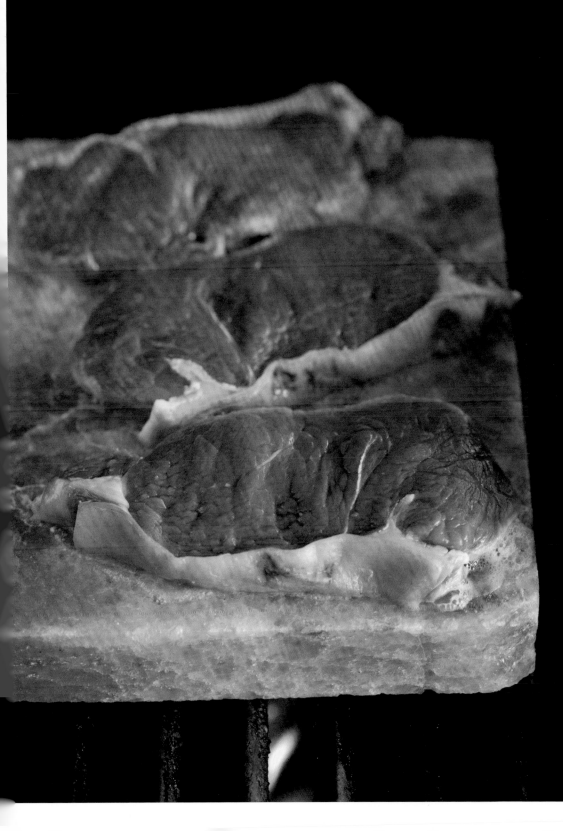

★ SALT BLOCK ★ OSTRICH BURGER

INGREDIENTS

500 g ostrich mince
1 onion, finely chopped
1 clove garlic, crushed
15 ml Worcestershire sauce
30 ml breadcrumbs
1 egg, beaten
salt and pepper
oil

Knead together the ostrich mince, onion, garlic, Worcestershire sauce, breadcrumbs, egg and seasoning. Shape the mince into 6 patties. Moisten with oil and refrigerate the patties for at least an hour to firm up.

Heat up the salt slab according to its instruction. The burger must sizzle when it hits the slab. Make a shallow indentation into each patty with your thumb to stop the burger from expanding in the centre. Put the ostrich burgers on the salt slab, dent side up, and close the lid. Braai for 2–3 minutes, then flip over. Braai for another 2 minutes.

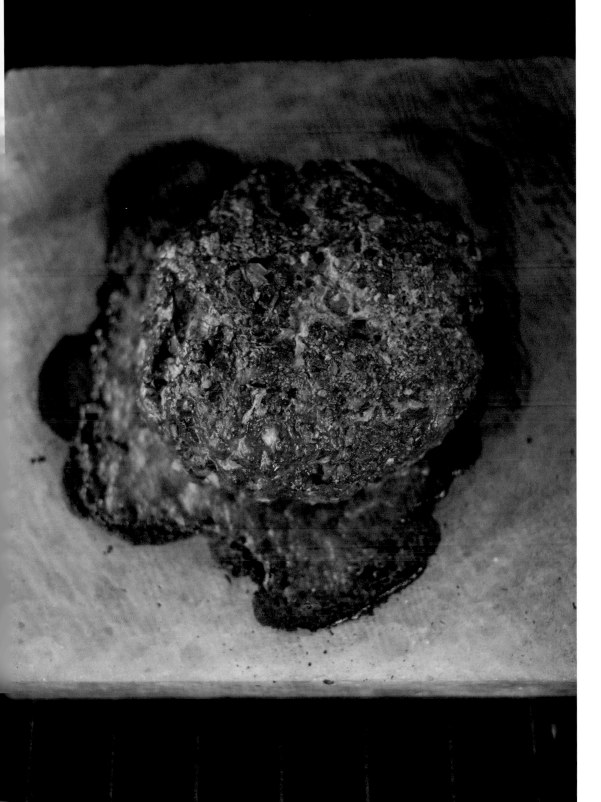

★ SALT BLOCK ★ ASPARAGUS ANGELS

INGREDIENTS

500 g fresh asparagus

12 pieces of streaky bacon

60 ml olive oil

freshly ground black pepper

WHOLE-GRAIN MUSTARD MAYO SAUCE

250 ml good quality mayonnaise

90 ml wholegrain mustard

15 ml lemon juice

salt and pepper

While the salt slab is heating up, mix the mayonnaise with the wholegrain mustard, lemon juice and seasoning in a small bowl and set aside.

Snap the tough ends off the asparagus and wrap each one in a piece of bacon (if they are a very thin, use two per bacon rasher). Brush the asparagus with olive oil and season with freshly ground black pepper.

Put the asparagus bundles on the hot salt slab, close the lid and braai until the bacon is crispy, about 3–4 minutes. The asparagus will turn a brighter green colour. Turn the bundles over, close the lid and braai on the other side for about 2 more minutes. Serve with the wholegrain mustard mayo sauce.

★ PLANKED ★ LAMB RACK

INGREDIENTS

2 x 300 g lamb racks
a herb brush
olive oil in a ramekin

SEASONING

250 ml salt
30 ml freshly ground black pepper
30 ml garlic salt
15 ml cayenne pepper

Combine seasoning ingredients in a small bowl. Transfer to a mortar and pestle, and grind to the consistency of sand. This stores in an airtight container for up to 3 months.

Bring the rack of lamb to room temperature an hour before the braai. Season the lamb with the seasoning blend to taste, then use your hands to rub it in. Allow to stand for the flavour to develop, and brush with a little olive oil before cooking.

Heat your gas braai to medium-high heat, and have your soaked plank of untreated wood near to hand. Brush the racks with olive oil from the ramekin using the herb brush.

Put the lamb racks down on the heated oiled grid for 2 minutes. Turn them over, brush again and braai for another 2 minutes. Repeat once more. Transfer the meat onto the soaked plank. Lean the racks against each other, bone end up. Close the lid and braai for 6–8 minutes. Transfer the rack of lamb to the dressing board. Let it rest for 3–4 minutes. To serve, slice the racks into chops, sprinkle with salt and more olive oil.

PLANKED PRAWNS
WITH HERBED BUTTER

INGREDIENTS

16 jumbo prawns

45 ml olive oil

60 ml fresh lemon juice

90 ml chopped chives or fennel

1 untreated plank, soaked in water for one hour

HERB BUTTER

60 ml fresh herbs, chopped, such as basil, dill or flat-leaf parsley

125 g unsalted butter, softened

salt and pepper

Beat the herbs into the softened unsalted butter and season with salt and pepper. Transfer to a small piece of greaseproof paper and roll into a log. Wrap the paper around the butter and twist the ends to seal. Refrigerate or freeze. Bring the herb butter to room temperature just before you braai the prawns.

Braaied prawns can be superb, but can be dry and tough too. Cooking them in their shells on a wet plank with some even heat rising off the plank can be one of the methods to ensure that the prawns are protected.

Cut the prawn shells down the back and devein the prawns. Leave the shell intact. Put the prawns into a bowl and marinate in olive oil and lemon juice for not longer than 10 minutes; otherwise the lemon juice will cook the prawn meat.

You need your gas braai on medium–high heat. Put the plank on the middle of the gas braai. Drain the prawns from the marinade. Pat dry lightly with paper towel. Put the prawns onto the plank, close the lid and braai for 6–8 minutes. Baste the prawns after 3 minutes with some herb butter. Close lid again. Prawns should be cooked opaque by now. Serve on the plank with the leftover herb butter on the side. Be sure your table is protected, as the underside of the plank will be very hot.

INGREDIENTS

4 X 200 g salmon fillet pieces

salt and pepper

The huge attraction of this method of cooking salmon is that it's really a conversation starter and it's very healthy. The oils in salmon are supposed to be very good for you, it's visually inviting, and there's much less fat in a fillet of Norwegian Salmon than on a lamb chop. It looks impressive too, but most of all, it's a really easy way to cook fish, even for those who think it an impossible task.

Cooking on the plank keeps it moist and, unless you get distracted watching the game for an hour, it won't burn.

Place your soaked plank on the grid over a medium heat. As the water begins to start evaporating, give it a very light brush of oil and pop the fish on it skin side down. I try to leave about 5 cm between each piece, so you might need two planks. Close the lid and cook for 4–5 minutes until the flesh turns pastel pink and starts to whiten slightly. If you really are a sucker for well done fish, leave it until the flesh starts to brown, but I warn you, it will be dry.

INGREDIENTS

1 whole fresh chicken

1 lemon, quartered

1 onion, chopped

1 apple, chopped

2 cloves garlic

small bunch of fresh sage, chopped

salt and pepper

120 ml olive oil

15 ml paprika

soaked kitchen string

Brine the chicken overnight if possible. See recipe for Brined Chicken on page 56.

Mix the lemon, onion, apple, garlic and sage in a bowl. Season and drizzle with some of the olive oil. Set aside.

Take the chicken out of the brine, rinse with cold water and set it on a chopping board. Stuff the chicken with the mixture. Tie the legs with the kitchen string. Rub olive oil over the chicken, and season with the salt, freshly ground black pepper and paprika.

Low heat is essential here so light only one side or set of burners to heat your smoke box. The chicken should not have a flame under it at all. Put your smoke box in place or use a cast iron pan or a foil package to hold the wood chips. Close the lid and smoke the chicken for 2 hours for a bird of around 1.2 kg. The skin will be stretched taut all over the bird by now; if it starts to curl away from the flesh, it's getting overdone and will dry out. There should still be a little give on the breast if you prod it with your finger.

★ SMOKED ★ DUCK

INGREDIENTS

4 leg and thigh duck pieces

4 very thin lemon slices, quartered

125 ml honey

juice of 2 lemons

15 ml salt

15 ml freshly ground black pepper

60 ml sesame oil

15 ml sesame seeds

5 ml flaked sea salt

Remove any excess fat from the duck pieces. Prick the skin all over with a fork. Put the duck in a colander and pour boiling water over it to encourage the subcutaneous fat to flow. Pat dry with some kitchen paper. Make 4 slashes or more in each thigh and insert the lemon slices, pushing them well in. Combine the honey, lemon juice, salt, freshly ground black pepper and sesame oil. Brush this glaze over the duck.

Heat your braai to the indirect method. Put smoke box in place. Place the duck in a foil container and place it away from the heat. Cover the lid and smoke for 20 minutes, then turn it over. Brush with remaining glaze and smoke the duck skin side up for 15 minutes.

Lightly toast the sesame seeds in a pan until lightly brown and mix with the salt flakes. Sprinkle the duck with the sesame seed salt and serve immediately.

SMOKED SALMON

INGREDIENTS

15 ml cooking oil

1 small side of salmon of 400 g

salt and pepper

steel chip box filled with wood chips

Set one burner on your braai to medium, and leave the other/s unlit. Place the smoke box on the grid over the lit burner to get it smoking.

As soon as it is smoking, turn the burner down to low and place the salmon on the oiled grid away from any flame or heat. Close the lid and leave it to smoke for roughly 20 minutes. The trick with the timing here is to learn when the fish is smoked by prodding it to assess the texture. It should be firm, like a cooked chicken breast.

I like to eat this with a fresh garden salad, it's a real treat.

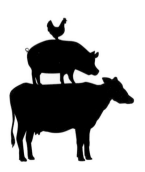

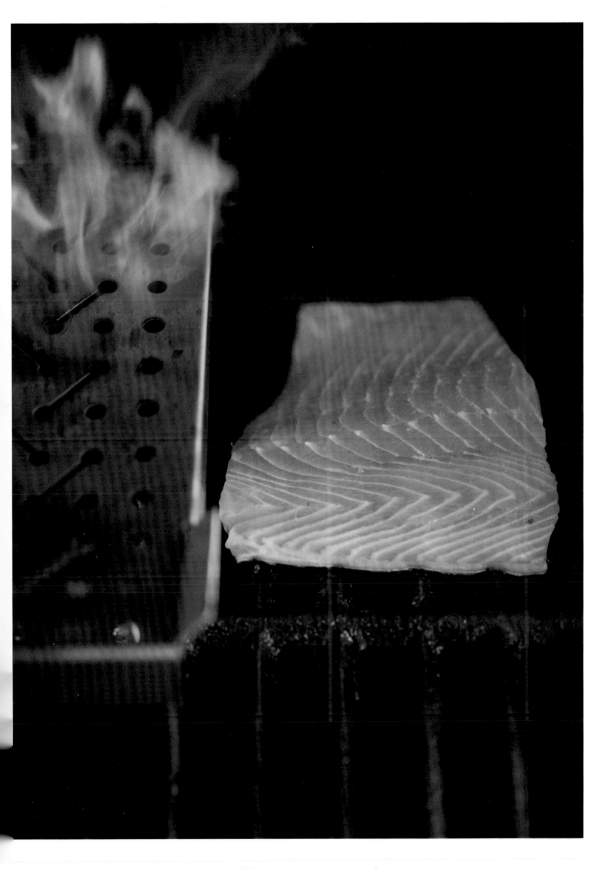

INGREDIENTS

1 whole chicken, spatchcocked

15 ml salt

5 ml freshly ground black pepper

5 ml cayenne pepper

15 ml olive oil

30 ml lemon zest, finely grated

30 ml fresh rosemary leaves

15 ml fresh thyme leaves

Place the chicken skin side up on a chopping board. Season all over with the salt and pepper, cayenne pepper and olive oil. Scatter the lemon zest, rosemary and thyme leaves over. Place in a baking dish and let stand at room temperature for an hour.

Heat a gas grill to medium. Brush braai grid with oil and place chicken, skin side down, on the grill. Place a foil-wrapped brick on top of chicken to weigh it down. Braai until skin is crispy, about 15 minutes.

Using braai tongs, set brick aside. Turn the chicken, replace the brick, close the lid and cook for a further 15 minutes. Remove the brick and check the chicken, turning it every 10 minutes until it is cooked through. The braai time should be between 45–50 minutes in total. Rest chicken for 10 minutes before serving.

UNDER A BRICK ★ SPRINGBOK

INGREDIENTS

1 springbok loin
a few sprigs of rosemary
8–10 rashers of streaky bacon
soaked kitchen string

MARINADE

1 small onion, finely chopped
2 garlic cloves, crushed
250 ml red wine
2 bay leaves
30 ml olive oil
30 ml soya sauce
juice of 1 orange
15 ml dried thyme
15 ml wholegrain mustard
peel of 1 orange

Sauté the onion and garlic until soft. Once cool, add the rest of the marinade ingredients. Put the springbok loin in a re-sealable bag, pour marinade over, seal and refrigerate overnight.

Remove the loin from the marinade. Place rosemary springs on the loin and wrap with the streaky bacon. Tie the loin with the soaked kitchen string.

Heat your gas braai to medium heat. Place the springbok loin on the braai grid and place the foil-wrapped brick on top. Close the lid and cook loin for 4–6 minutes. Using braai tongs, set the brick aside. Turn the loin over, replace the brick and braai for 2–3 minutes. The braai time should be between 9 and 12 minutes. Rest the meat for 10 minutes before carving.

INGREDIENTS

16 whole calamari tubes,
cleaned

DRESSING

15 ml salt

15 ml freshly ground black
pepper

15 ml chopped garlic

60 ml lemon juice, freshly
squeezed

90 ml olive oil

BACKYARD SALSA

12 baby tomatoes, halved

1 red onion, chopped finely

1 avocado, cubed

1 red chilli, deseeded and
chopped

45 ml coriander leaves, finely
chopped

75 ml fresh lemon juice

60 ml olive oil

Combine all salsa ingredients in a bowl and set aside.
Combine all the dressing ingredients in a bowl, toss in
the calamari and leave it for 20 minutes.

Prepare your braai for direct cooking on a high heat and
make sure your grid is very clean. Arrange the calamari
tubes so they fit under a brick (6–8 to a brick). You can
use 2 bricks if you are feeding many. I always add the
little tentacle bits and fill the spaces in between the tubes
with those; they turn into nice crunchy bits. Braai for
2 minutes with the lid closed. Wearing braai gloves, tilt
the bricks and turn the calamari tubes. Place the bricks
on top of the calamari again and braai for a further
minute or 2. Repeat method with the remaining calamari
tubes. Serve the calamari on top of the salsa on a platter.

Calamari onl

Calamari + chip

Calamari
only 45

★ SEAFOOD POTJIE ★

INGREDIENTS

30 ml butter

30 ml olive oil

3 celery stalks, finely chopped

1 large onion, finely diced

4 cloves garlic, crushed

30 ml fish spice

410 g tinned tomatoes

1 bay leaf

juice and zest of 2 lemons

125 ml dry white wine

500 ml vegetable stock

1 kg black mussels, cleaned
and scrubbed

250 g prawns, shelled and
deveined

500 g hake fillets, cut into
chunks

250 g calamari rings

15 ml corn flour

125 ml cream

60 ml fresh basil, torn

90 ml fresh parsley, chopped

Heat your gas braai to medium-high heat. Place a cast iron pot on the gas braai. Heat up for 10 minutes and add the butter and oil into it. Add the celery, onions and garlic and fry for a few minutes. Add fish spice. Fry for a minute. Add the tomato, bay leaf, lemon juice, lemon zest, white wine and vegetable stock. Let it simmer for 15–20 minutes uncovered. Add the mussels, prawns, hake fillet and calamari rings. Turn your gas braai to a high heat. Cook until the mussels open. While the seafood is cooking, mix the corn flour with the cream. Stir into the pot and turn the heat down to medium. Let the pot simmer for 5 minutes or until sauce has thickened. Season again and add fresh basil and parsley.

INGREDIENTS

30 ml olive oil

4 lamb shanks

salt and pepper

4 garlic cloves, peeled

4 medium-sized carrots, chopped

2 celery sticks, sliced

2 onions, peeled and chopped

1 bottle red wine

250 ml water

2 bay leaves

4 black peppercorns

15 ml thyme

15 ml rosemary

Preheat your braai to medium-high heat. Place a cast iron pot onto your gas braai and let it heat up for 5 minutes. Heat the olive oil in the pot. Season the lamb shank with salt and pepper and brown them on all sides in the hot oil. This should take no longer than 5 minutes. Add the garlic cloves, carrots, celery and onion to the pot. Stir meat and vegetables for 2 minutes. Add the red wine and let the wine boil for 3–5 minutes. Add the water, bay leaves, peppercorns and fresh herbs. Turn your gas braai down to low. Cover the cast iron pot with a lid. Turn the gas braai down to a medium heat. Close the braai lid. Cook the lamb shanks in the potjie for 90 minutes or until tender, stirring once when cooking. Transfer the lamb shanks to a dish. Keep warm. Strain the sauce by pressing it through a fine sieve. Boil the liquid over high heat until reduced to 375 ml. Spoon the sauce over the lamb shanks and serve.

★ ACKNOWLEDGEMENTS ★

Nina Talliard, look how things panned out after your first article in a Cape Town newspaper so many years ago!

Abigail Donnelly, I value your friendship, support and guidance, and deeply respect your tenacity. Your work as a stylist, editor and food pioneer has been a constant inspiration to me (and to all South Africans) over the years.

Maurizio Grossi – grazie mille, dankie, thank you! You are an integral part of this wonderful story and the journey I have travelled to tell it.

Sheryl Ozinsky, people should learn from you how to put an event together. Thank you for all the National Braai Day events and for your part in inspiring the Braai Nation to eat and live better.

Fiona Mckie, our hunt to find the perfect rib-eye steak has been a journey full of laughter, fun good times and lots of love. Clean the braai, Fifi!

Niell Grobler and Chase Weir, let's light the fire on your next visit to Cape Town! Thank you for arranging those Weber beauties we used to cook for this book.

Ryan Boon is a wonderful supplier to work with. He is a butcher in the true sense of the word, carrying a torch for a dying craft as vital to the braai as matches. All the beautiful red meat for this book came from Ryan Boon Meats.

My humble thanks to my clients, food suppliers and all who have supported me on this journey. No matter how small the service or favour, it has all contributed to this wonderful thing I do for a living.

To my staff, Dean MacDonald, Shanaaz Cassie, Melanie Pietersen, Rachel Chitsa and Lindelwa Ndunge for braaiing in rain, wind or sunshine. You guys rock.

To my beloved Webers, you never question me, you just click into action and make things happen. You always bring the flame.

Lastly, enormous thanks are due to my publisher Russel Wasserfall, for his friendship and astute professional observation. The fact that he is capable of this as well as shooting such beautiful images of my food makes me proud that he has invested so much effort in my work. We make a formidable team when we Braai the Beloved Country.

★ INDEX ★

First published by Russel Wasserfall Food,
an imprint of Jacana Media (Pty) Ltd, in 2015
Second impression 2015

10 Orange Street
Sunnyside
Auckland Park 2092
South Africa
+2711 628 3200
www.jacana.co.za

ISBN 978-1-928247-04-3

Design by Shawn Paikin
Recipe development and styling - Jean Nel
Photography, art direction, styling - Russel Wasserfall
Kitchen production - Derek Moore
Set in Stempel Garamond and Trade Gothic
Printed and bound by Creda Communications
Job no. 002460

Also available as an e-book:
d-PDF 978-1-928247-05-0

See a complete list of Jacana titles at www.jacana.co.za